To Cat any friend of Mary-Ellen's ...

Making Hay

Noodling by Diana McLellan
Doodling by Peter Steiner

... with warmest regards.

[signature]

XOX
Sept 10, 2012

Booktrope Editions
Seattle, Washington
2012

Cover Design by Victoria Wolffe
Cover Drawing by Peter Steiner

ISBN 978-1-935961-48-2

DISCOUNTS OR CUSTOMIZED EDITIONS MAY BE AVAILABLE
FOR EDUCATIONAL AND OTHER GROUPS BASED ON BULK
PURCHASE.

For further information please contact info@booktrope.com.

Library of Congress Control Number: 2012913124

Noodlings

Part 4   Making Hay

CONFESSIONS

Yes, I'm corny – from my bottom to my heart, as a little girl once said. Who writes about hearts, at my age?

But love persists. Bottoms persist. Life amazes. Death waits. Dreams soar, swoop, shake and rattle. Sometimes I feel like an Australian aborigine, whose sacred dream-time (Altjeringa) is more important than his daily grind. (See "Two Meetings.")

I'm nosy, too. I wonder what urban writer friends get up to when they retreat to their "farms" on weekends - hence "Making Hay." I puzzle over what mice, which scientists recently found sing to each other high above human earshot, have to sing about. They also weep copiously while mating. (Mice, not scientists.) Do they know something we don't?

You'll find some oddities. "Cross with Hugo Williams" is a note I faxed to that poet when he brazenly announced in his TLS column that he'd written a non-rhyming villanelle. (After a rude initial response, he eventually told me he'd stuck my admonition in his scrapbook. His villanelle is grand.) "Leave Me My Rags" materialized the day a burglar hit our old house, making off with two very fine mink coats that a friend had inherited from her mother and passed on to me. Piled near our drafty front door, they gave the intruder the impression that we were enormously rich. He ransacked everything from my disgraceful ragbag to our battered old boxes of Christmas decorations, hunting our artfully-hidden diamonds. I think he left feeling sorry for us.

You'll note outbreaks of the fantods. Offerings like "A Scottish Lament" "Cracked Bell" and "Diagnosis: Dragons" are definitely downers. But before you send gin or chocolates, know that my gloom-clouds blow over quite fast.

Minor explanations: Rue, the bitter herb, was called the Herb of Grace because pre-Reformation English priests used it to sprinkle holy water on their (probably quite ripe) congregations. The Norfolk I refer to is the English county, home of my mother's family for many generations. And Bumpass is a town in Virginia, once famed for its wooden ice-cream spoon factory. I love the name. Welcome to my little world. And thanks to my favorite artist/cartoonist (and author) Peter Steiner for joining me here.

--DIANA MCLELLAN

RICHARD!

PART I
Breakfast with a Squirrel

A SMALL BEGINNING

Listen. A black dog howls at dawn.
Chained to his stake the sun-mad day,
Muzzled, neglected, starved, forlorn,
He strains to snap at phantom prey.

What great crow beats its heavy wings
Circling and screaming all day long -
Cawing of carrion, wasted things,
Sick heart, spent treasure, silent song?

But here's what you don't want to hear:
There is a gnat that wails at night,
Stinging, but singing in your ear
A thin, high song of morning light.

THREE SCORE AND TEN

What is age, when your body cannot tell the time?
When you're biking, you're ten. Maybe twenty when
    swimming.
In dreams, thirty-five - my Tallulah's alive -
Around forty with wineglasses clinking and brimming.
At dinner by candlelight, loving, or walking,
Your heart's pleasured rhythm won't beat itself old;
Your friends are so beautiful while they are talking
That you must be, too, 'til you're coffined and cold.
Do you have some small gifts? Envy will not revoke them,
Nor mockery shrink, nor old rivals diminish.
Delights dwell within. Honest thought will provoke them,
And memory's music is yours, 'til the finish.

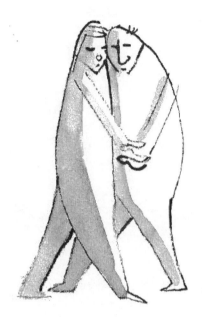

OLDER WOMAN

He said I was too old for him
When I was all of twenty-three;
Now fifty years have come and gone -
And he is far too old for me.

ADVICE TO A VERY YOUNG MAN

When you wake up brand-new each day,
Just meet the world the grown-up way!
Show Mom and Dad you know what's what -
And always poo-poo in the pot!

Then when it's nap-time at your school,
Just keep your pants Buzz-Lightyear cool.
Now don't be shy! Head for that spot!
And always, poo-poo in the pot.

And after lunch, each afternoon,
Smell nice, and keep your world in tune.
And always give it your best shot -
Make sure you poo-poo in the pot!

When nighttime comes, and time for bed,
You've lots of wisdom in your head.
You know just where to go, where not -
So always, poo-poo in the pot!

MORE ADVICE FOR A VERY
YOUNG MAN

Grady, Grady: Open your pie-hole, do.
There's some lady trying to feed you goo.
It isn't a snake or lizard,
Ground up to gag your gizzard,
So open wide,
And pack inside
Something tasty that's great for you.

INVITATION

You say your juice ran out? Well here I am,
Shrunken inside my antique storage jar,
Reduced to sticky essence, like old jam
Shelved where the anchovies and nutmeg are.
Maybe what's left fermented – vintage wine,
Vinegar-puckered, spiced with years and
    pain;
Together, we can sample yours and mine,
Then, drunken, reel into the world again.
There's not much time. And what there is will
    send
Into the night where you and I must fall
Craven and brave alike. Before the end
Join me for cocktails, kindest hour of all –
Six-thirty sharp. Take taxis. Don't be late.
Who knows when we can keep another date?

BREAKFAST WITH
A SQUIRREL

Black branches spike against a pewter sky.
Mist drapes the silent landscape like a shroud;
Old leaves blow broken, derelict and dry.

But by my window, scrambling, leaping high,
An acrobat, gray as a thundercloud,
Sails limb to limb against the pewter sky

Harvesting twig-tip seeds. Oh, he can fly,
Then snatch, sway, dangle - perilously proud,
High over dead leaves, derelict and dry.

One tiny hand misplaced, and he will die
While I, his heart-in-gullet circus crowd,
Will watch him plummet past the pewter sky.

My hand against the glass has caught his eye.
His breakfast's over. Sated, twitch-tailed, cowed,
He flees. Old leaves blow derelict and dry.

Simply to live, he leaps. And so must I
Forgo a safety-net, nor scold aloud.
Black branches spike against the pewter sky;
Old leaves blow broken, derelict and dry.

CRACKED BELL

The heart tolls deep inside -
Cracked bell of stone.
Low wit and high-stakes pride
Ring rough, alone.
And now, as short days stalk
The endless night,
Soft echoes, gentle talk,
Can't ring it right.

FRIEND OF MY CHILDHOOD

Friend of my childhood, do not die.
It's much too soon -
The sun has barely scorched the sky.
This afternoon
Let's play Bad Dog 'til we cry with laughter
And sing our song,
Eat jam, turn cartwheels, get sick after,
And swim too long,
Then three-legged race to the climbing-tree
Down by the sand,
After donkey-rides, spend the night with me
And hold my hand.
We'll midnight-feast on stolen pie
And watch the moon.
Friend of my childhood, do not die.
Too soon. Too soon.

MISSING

The full moon hides behind the rain.
Black is the night; opaque the skies.
When will I see your face again,
And glimpse the light beyond your
      eyes?

NIGHTLIFE NOW

At night you slip into the past
Where unlived lives and loves abide.
You can reshake the die uncast,
And spill it on another side.

After the long quotidian day
The heart still leaps, the tears still flow
For best-loved faces, turned away.
Now, they can call. And you can go.

A GIRL LIKE I

Girlhood androgyny's divine,
Our later roles, unpickable.
A woman's work is fun and fine
When it's not too despicable;
Her brain may sing the party line -
Her heart is inexplicable.

Now I believe in yang and ying
And animus and anima.
The boy-girl vive la difference thing
Obtains from Minsk to Panama.
Without it, no more kids. No zing
To paintings, books or cinema.

Our first decade was perfect joy.
Then, forty years of hormone hell -
Part queen, part whore, part Mum, part toy.
Then, late-life tangos start to swell.
"No more man-woman, girl-and-boy!"
We cheer. Ignore that funny smell.

VALENTINE FROM CRAMPED QUARTERS

The walnut crams its sculptured shell,
The fly fills up its amber tomb,
Rich honey brims the waxen cell,
And baby's snug within the womb;
The stone's held tight inside the peach,
Eggshells encase life's pulsing start,
The sea enfolds the whale's great breach -
Just so, my darling crowds my heart.

THE SHELLS

When I am not a part of him and he is not a part of me
My heart's an empty cockleshell a thousand miles from any sea
When I can't scale the stony cliff that rears between, too steep to
     gain,
My heart's a chambered nautilus, white-dry as bones bleached on a
     plain
Though leaden clouds blot out the sun and darkness wraps them
     deep inside,
My seashells know the moon is high. They clink with every turning
     tide.

OLD LOVE

Old love is autumn's last red rose,
Velvet and fragrant in your hand.
Old love is winter's early snows,
White-dazzling on the dying land.
Old love's a lustrous green-glass sea
That washes time beyond the tide -
Old love's a sunset, gilding me
So all about is glorified.

WHEN IT'S MY TURN

When it's my turn to rush toward the light,
I'll pack my pockets tightly for the run
And squeeze among bright scraps of past delight,
Epiphanies and moments in the sun
The love of friends and other loves I've known;
Beauty of waters, trees and streets and skies;
A kiss of fame; ecstatic work alone;
Familiar chatter; music; laughing eyes;
Small children's trusting hands; all questing
    talks,
Old women's wisdom; swimming turquoise sea;
Stars, wine and candles after winter walks;
Joy in the blood - all these, I'll take with me.
Back on sweet earth's beloved pulsing heap
I'll leave betrayal, guile, and pain - to sleep.

SUSURRATION

The leaves are clinging to their boughs
Although November's growing old -
Presenting, as the chill wind soughs,
Singing bouquets of red and gold.

What is their ballad, soft and long,
Serenading the cold pearl sky?
Their time is past, is all their song.
Soon they must go. And so must I.

PART II
Eclipse by Candlelight

VERY FLAT, NORFOLK

In Norfolk, where my family lived forever,
A euphemism's not considered clever.
All talk is sharpened to a point, and baleful;
Loose women "will suck sorrow by the pailful."
No man will share his skills, nor will he show:
"Oy just in't goin' to give them all moy know."
Slummocking mawthers (fat girls) lollop past,
And talk rum squit, if courteously arst.
"All of a muckwash" - sweatiness defined;
And rough chapped hands are "like a bear's behind."
Flat land; flat prospects; flat the Ouse's flow.
No kisses parting. Just, "Mind how you go."
That bitter rain-drenched wind is "rafty weather."
Cover your lugs, and come you on together.

RAGS OF MEMORY

Leave me my rags of memory, Burglar Time -
Enough to understand what past I own,
To piece my thoughts, unseemly or sublime,
And quilt small scraps from garments long
        outgrown.
Cutting my ragbag's dusty humdrum strings
I root for truth in sackcloth and brocade,
Fish deep inside the linty mess of things,
To sort out what I've torn from what I've made:
Here's tattered cashmere, feathers, real silk hose,
Buttons snipped off, old trimmings ripped in
        haste,
Cotton and satin; leather; velvet rose,
Ribbons too worn to show, too good to waste.
Come age, come pain, come death - Thief, load
        your bags,
But spare my memory's bright tangled rags.

BABY THROUGH THE WALL

I hear a baby wailing through the wall -
Piercing, persistent, not to be denied;
Surely my heart will not respond at all.

And yet there is a tug, a full recall,
An elemental force that has not died.
I hear a baby wailing through the wall.

Nursing! The thought has no appeal. Appall
Is closer to the mark, at end-of-ride;
Surely my heart will not respond at all -

I'd just as soon sign up for basketball.
But somehow, tender reflexes abide:
I hear a baby wailing through the wall.

Why do I rise to meet a newborn's squall,
Helpless, compelled, as moonlight swells the tide?
Surely my heart will not respond at all.

Old age's consolations are on call:
Detachment from the flesh, and peace, and pride.
I hear a baby wailing through the wall.
Surely, my heart will not respond at all.

CROSS WITH HUGO WILLIAMS

A poet who writes a villanelle,
And proudly boasts "It does not rhyme,"
Deserves to fry in Poets' Hell.

He's like a clock that won't tell time,
A vintner who can't taste or smell,
A talking, squawking, painted mime,

Oeufs en gelée that did not jell,
A brand-new dress-shirt smudged with grime,
A case of mumps that failed to swell,

A margarita sans the lime,
A runny cheese with no ripe smell,
A diamond from the five-and-dime.

Just stop and think. And then pray tell
Exactly what you think is prime
About a rhymeless villanelle?

Ideally, two rhymes are swell;
Three, less than perfect, but no crime.
Suppose it scans, but does not rhyme?
Art, maybe. Not a villanelle.

RECIPES

If I were young and lovely
I'd steal those sky-blue eyes.
I'd thickly brush with corn-meal mush
And roll them in an herbal crush
To fry some gazin' pies.

If I were young and lovely
I'd snatch that thumping heart.
I'd knit it sleeves of lovage leaves
And pepper it, to ward off thieves,
And bake my cheri tart.

If I were young and lovely,
I'd squeeze that singing soul;
Whisked up supreme with honeyed cream
I'd slurp its rich delicious stream
From Madame's silver bowl.

ECLIPSE BY CANDLELIGHT

As the silent night creeps dawnward and the weary year grows
 older
And the full moon slithers, copper-tinged, into the cat-black shade,
It's not moon, nor blazing torchiere in a gilded-silver holder,
But a slender wavering flame that lights the little lives we've made.

PART III
View from a Tidal Pool

THE HERB OF GRACE

It burgeoned first, the morning glory vine
That twined about my gate, blue trumpet-flowered;
Then blew the lemon tree, as dark as wine,
Starred with white blossoms, swelling fruit that soured.
Now droops the willow, mourning by a stream,
Its supple branches lashed by summer's gale;
Then mistletoe, some oak's Druidic dream
Turns sacrificial, languorous and pale.
Mystical mushrooms burst the earth around
And spray spored visions, blowing past the years -
And finally, up through the harsh gray ground
Springs rue, the Herb of Grace, to scatter tears.

DYING IN COMPANY,
PLEASINGLYATTIRED

Imagine, now, our time has come to die,
Together, on a couch of softest down.
On starched white sheets, cool to the touch,
    we lie.

No T-shirts! Blue pajamas, piped in brown,
Of silk, for you. And at your side am I.
And I am wearing - what? A white silk gown?

Crisp lace-trimmed linen ruffles, with a tie?
An orange prison jumpsuit and a frown?
On starched white sheets, cool to the touch,
    we lie.

Black leather? Vinyl? Rubber? Lamé? My
Attire must work for country or for town,
For heaven or hell, or where our spirits fly.

Antique kimono? Slinky satin? Crown?
Your momma's fuzzy bathrobe? (Don't be
    shy!)
Sprigged muslin nightie? Motley, like a
    clown?

Please circle firmly that which might apply.
Remember, now, our time has come to die -
And we will kiss before we say goodbye.
On starched white sheets, cool to the touch,
    we lie.

PRAYER FOR A NEIGHBOR

There is a fool up on a roof.
Sweet Jesus, guide his feet.
Don't let that goof seek manhood's proof
So coffin-worms might eat.

As carpenter and Christ, you bore
The hammer's theft of ease.
Dear Lord, restore that poor guy's sore
Rotator cuff and knees.

And should a foot be wrongly put
And he go plunging down,
May he survive, dumb but alive,
Insured. God save the clown.

EVENINGS WITH FRIENDS

Biking beside the leafy park
I turned my head.
Surely I saw my darling Clark?
No. He is dead.
In Georgetown - twice! - I almost hailed
Roy, for the joy his music gave;
Then, as blunt memory prevailed,
Gazed at his grave.
Robin and Charlie, Dave and John
Laughed candlelit in my dim rooms;
Maria, Sharkey, Mike - long gone
To unlit tombs.
Friends of my heart, you're with me still
As evening falls.
Your presence lights, and always will,
My night-dark walls.

LOSS

The moon that swelled the tide has gone,
The lamp-lit rain that sang of sleep;
The dawn that gilded where it shone;
Star-glittered waters' mirrored deep.
Quenched now the embers' dying glow,
Snuffed out the torch that lit my way.
All brightness that the earth could show
Has dimmed. Now, darkness and decay.

A SHORTAGE OF REGRETS

The years are racing by so fast
And I am growing old at last,
With limited tomorrows.
So should I sigh for what I've missed -
Those hands unheld, those lips unkissed -
Or cheer for smaller sorrows?

Suppose I skipped some keen delights –
Short laughing days, long tender nights
And strange souls intertangled?
Love such a heavy forfeit takes
In payment for the ale and cakes.
Old hearts thump best unmangled.

SPELL FOR A SICK FRIEND

O let me fly to nestle
In the cockles of his heart,
Like an oval sun-lapped pebble
In a tidal pool apart.
Let my carol lilt and rustle
Through his lonely halls at night -
My calypso through his castle
Dapple languor with delight.
Let me paddle though his vessels,
Bubble healing through his blood,
Jostle pain until it's docile,
Wrestle with his vital flood,
Wheedle through his soul's sealed portal,
Whistle trills to lure what's mortal,
And trample febrile fardels in the mud.

THE INTRUDER

Have you tapped me yet, Death, with your
    safecracker's finger?
Did you case my small mansion and jimmy its door?
While I sleep do you creep to my bed? Do you linger
To prod my false stillness, to sniff at my snore?
Do you pad to the tick-tocking clock of my heart,
Pick the lock that unlatches its pulsing red gate -
Tease thin wires through my veins, probe the flimsiest
    part,
And amusedly scratch at a site for our date?
Have you coiled through my bowels? Sucked my
    shallow night breath?
Kissed my breast like a lover? Sown seed in my womb?
Notched a niche in my brain for decay, sly old Death,
So I'll follow you, babbling, out of the room?

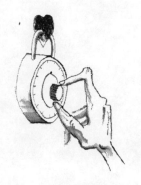

COUP DE VIEUX

The night he left her heart,
Lead filled her feet, dank sulfur soured her breath,
Night swallowed sun, like death,
The night they moved apart.

The day he turned aside,
Brain shriveled, eyes decayed, lips paled, new-dead,
Light shadowed, pleasure fled,
Washed out past any tide.

The year he turned snow-cold,
Chill struck into her entrails, ice her bones,
Blood stilled, song died. Heart moans
That suddenly, she's old.

THE VISITOR

One dank bedraggled February day
Our ninety-year-old neighbor, Kathryn Noel,
Who plied religious tracts we threw away,
Emerged from her dim basement like a mole
Blinking at chilly sunshine. There she found
Carpets of crocus, radiant, purple-dyed,
Starred altar cloths spread on the scrubby
    ground.
"Look what my God has given me," she cried,
Warming her blue-veined hands inside her
    sleeves.
(Maybe kind Mary Wyman - other side -
Had slipped brown corms beneath last year's
    dead leaves.)
"A miracle," I said. We gazed, embraced,
Marveled and laughed. Then, twenty years
    marched by.
Her garden and her self have been replaced
By glamorous newcomers. And yet I,
Still, every February, greet croci
Which - brilliant resurrection - pierce the sere,
Announcing Mrs. Noel's God was here.

A SCOTTISH LAMENT

My heart is like the gray-black rock, the jagged rock
That's drowned beneath the icy loch, the dark-blue loch -
Flung from the shore by helpless hand, by feckless hand,
To lie half-frozen, out of sight and far from land.

Goodbye for aye, my aching heart, my dying heart
It's long past time to weep and part, forever part.
Without you there's no warming pain, no beating pain,
And we shall never dream we're angels, not again.

PART IV
Making Hay

MAKING HAY

O my darling is a country man,
He hunts, he grunts, he swears;
He hones his knives, he sights his guns,
He chases off the bears.
He snores a bit, he whores a bit,
And at the end of day
He's out naked in the moonlight
With his pitchfork, making hay.

O my darling is a writing man
On matters glum and gay.
A-groaning at his word machine,
Brow furrowed, legs asplay,
His mind's as deep as Hades' holes
And wider than the Bay,
And he's naked in the moonlight
With his pitchfork, making hay.

GET-WELL CARD

Now, I would take your pain -
At least a bit of it.
I'd sacrifice some brain
To have you quit of it.
I'd gently touch your ache
(I've healing hands, it's said,)
And through my fingers, take
Your misery to my bed.
I'd feed you savory stews,
And offer warmth or ice,
Then, quietly amuse,
Now, mightn't that be nice?

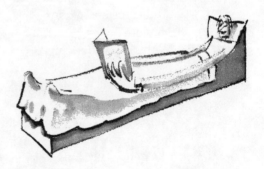

NO SMELLS NO BELLS

Suppose harsh words were spoken or unspoken -
Our lives untangled, ardent hearts grown cold?
Sometimes they do. Suppose my own was broken?
Pain beyond pain. Then, dying, very old,
I'd wonder just what scent there might have been,
Unsoaped, unshaven, seedy, worked, unclean.
Sharp like a cheese, or roadkill deer? Soft yeast?
Like goat or hen-house, eel-skin, wildebeest?
Comforting, homely, like a grandma's bed?
Or sweaty-soft, a summer baby's head?
Garlic-exuding? Mutton-suet ripe,
Sweet, sour, or woodbine-fragrant, old-man's-pipe?
Without true scent, affection's like a stone -
Loss needs a perfume it can call its own.

BIRTHDAY MEMORIES FOR TARA

Here you are, red, with wide-flung arms, new-born -
Puzzled but pleased by the strange German view.
Even the childbirth-hardened stiff-lipped nun
Smiled at the gallant soul that leapt in you.
Days later, sick and hot inside your room,
Still, uncomplaining, thoughtfully you lay,
Gazing expectantly into the gloom,
Certain and glad that help was on its way.
Your hips were out of joint; a cast applied -
Was it a year until they set in place? -
Confined, you scooted crabwise to the side,
Delighted with yourself, the human race.
At two or three, you'd sleep in our old house,
Watch "Wizard," bathe, then share your secret woes:
"Oomi, is there such things as toe-monsters,
Under the bed, that wait to eat my toes?
My Uncle Donald says so." "No, he's wrong."
Gravely you nodded. Then we turned to song.
"Sing Jingle Bells and rub my tummy, please."
Dirge-slow I sang and rubbed. You laughed, then
    slept.
Mornings, your small form scrambled to our nest,
And seal-like slipped between us 'til we rose.
The honor! Cartoons flickered through our rest
As though an angel fanned our dawn repose.
Breakfast was met with rapturous acclaim:
"Did you make this for me?" Beloved child.
There was the morning of the Wooden Spoon
You grabbed to bang each dangling pan, half-wild -
Godawful racket, joy enough to swoon,
Capering, laughing. Round the Hill we strayed;
You walked low walls, swung trusting from our
    arms;
Listened entranced as street-musicians played.

The circus! Hurrying to its riotous charms
Granddad and I, each holding one small hand,
Felt, as the music crackled through the night
Ecstatic current, skipping toward the band.
Tara means "Star" in Sanskrit. How'd they know?
At nursery school, the Photo: Your great show.
Secretly, in your Little Pony tin
You hid the diamonds, lipstick, eyelid-blue.
Our star! At least they let you wear the pin.
"She's like a flame," one teacher said of you.
And so, you flared in grace. And still you do.

INVITATION FROM A CITY MOUSE

Princess of mice! Come, now that winter's due.
Here, servants scatter crumbs around the floor
In my great city palace. Start anew!
Next to the stove we'll sprinkle fragrant spoor.
With happy tears we'll mate, then mate some more.
Gay sensate spray of whiskers! Dawn-pink feet!
Translucent mushroom ears! Eyes black as fleas!
Brisk twitching haunches, sinuous scented tail!
Teats close-arrayed to suckle hordes of wees!
Inside our castle's cozy sofa, drag
Torn paper, feathers, fuzz, soft cleaning-rag.

Our sires sang hymns in praise of ripened grain,
Vast habitable banquets, sun-soaked stacks,
Red barns, mouse-heavens, sheltered from the rain.
But danger lurks there - cat and fox attacks,
Cruel knife-clawed badgers; slithering starveling
    things.
Outside, great taloned raptors gyre to strike
Grandma and suckling, sick and spry alike -
Falcon and eagle, raven, hawk and shrike
Silence our sweet al fresco carolings.
My pretty: Come to town! Here, breed at ease,
Singing urbane duets of love and cheese.

ADVICE FROM NORFOLK

When I was young and gay
My mother used to say
When I'd crave some future day, "Love,
Don't wish your life away,
Don't wish your life away."

And now I'm on the wane
And I've had a whiff of pain
I can hear her voice again: "Love,
You'd better dress for rain.
You'd better dress for rain."

GREETINGS TO A GREAT-GRANDSON

Welcome to Earth, new, much-loved ginger lad.
And, darling of my darlings: Meet the sun!
That rumbling racket's thunder - not too bad;
Consider it your drum roll, precious one.
And is your soul aboard, where it can grow?
And are your hungers in their proper place?
And have your fingers splayed? And do you know
Your mother's waiting breast, her sweet young face?
Child of the brave new world: No looking back
Can cloud your memory's fresh, still-sleeping eye.
But yet, your feet may stray upon my track,
And I'll know you, you me, before I die.

DIAGNOSIS: DRAGONS

So. Now we drift into uncharted seas
Where sucking whirlpools churn beneath the gray
And monsters writhe through snaking seaweed trees
To caverns where they gnaw their undead prey.
There is no lifeboat here to brave the tide;
No god or mermaid dives to purge the lairs.
Let us be graceful as we're clawed inside,
And staunch those choking craven bootless prayers.
Perhaps a glimpse of daybreak through the gloom -
Corpse-pallid in the sickened greenish night –
Reveals one fond familiar in the room
Pointing a trembling finger to the light
Or gurgling greetings to the newest guest.
Here there be dragons. We must do our best.

THE WIDOW'S RESOLUTION

I will be happy, happy as a hen
Sitting upon six hard-boiled eggs for weeks,
Certain that soon her hatchlings will begin
Tapping their tiny lifeward-thrusting beaks.

I will be happy, happy as a nun
Or blood-soaked Aztec priest at morning prayer:
Dim cell or staring sacrificial sun
Suffused with knowledge that a god will care.

I will be happy, happy as a trout
Mounting green light toward the glittering fly,
Slipping through ardent water, leaping out
To thrash against the radiant air and die.

THE GREEDY LOVER

Beauty and fame both soon expire,
And so does art.
I don't care how much you admire.
I want your heart -
Spontaneous as rain, brush-fire,
Or errant fart.
Mine's yours - I think - and won't require
Some missing part.
So, gravid with my rich desire
I'll sulk, apart.

MY LOVELY LAUGHING FRIENDS

My lovely laughing friends have died
Or moved into the place called Pain.
And though I hold their wit like gold
Their coins won't clink or glint again.

The years stretch on. Still I abide.
I'll join them in a little while.
Each day, I take more time to wake.
At night, we often share a smile.

THE BUMPASS BLUES

Git up in the mornin', boil up my grits in the pail;
They oldy and they moldy, but they better'n that slop I et in jail.
Got the Bumpass Blues, yeah, bluer than a Star Kist tuna can,
'Cos my baby done skedaddle with that bug-eyed DC Cable TV man.

Lord, my teeth are turnin' yeller; my eyes are red, my hair's a catfish
    gray,
And my heart's all swole and purple, cos it's stomped on every night
    and every day.
Got the Bumpass Blues, yeah, bluer than a Ty-D-Bol round,
'Cos my baby, she done run off with that bug-eyed DC Cable TV
    hound.

It's rainin' in my outhouse, soakin' through my catalog from Sears.
I just bought me ten new dishrags, but they never gonna dry my
    streamin' tears.
Got the Bumpass Blues, yeah, bluer than a Hooters cutie's eye
'Cos my baby she done lef' me, for that bug-eyed DC Cable TV guy.

Lord, my ears are stiff and salty, cos I lay in bed and cry myself a
    river,
Drinkin' musseltail with moonshine 'til my brain's as sick with mis'ry
    as my liver.
Got the Bumpass Blues, yeah, bluer than Viagra in a jar,
'Cos my baby done skedaddle in that bug-eyed DC Cable man's slick
    car.

FOR A PERFECT NAP
AFTER AN EXCELLENT SWIM

Kind god of slumber, to my sofa creep
To wreathe with poppies chlorine-tangled hair.
Where sorrows splash in currents green and deep
By Lethe's banks, spiced Lotos draughts prepare-
Spread silken shrouds, enfold the half-day's care,
And drug my sated senses into sleep.

AFTER A VISIT FROM A GREAT GRANDSON

This life is short. These latter parts,
When twilight falls and darkness
    looms,
Urge us to open wide our hearts,
And wander though their shuttered
    rooms.
So let's embrace what we adore-
Our secret dreams, our soul's desires-
Root out what lurks beneath our store,
Our golden glints, our dreaming spires,
And give, as long as we can give,
To loves who barely know we live.

TWO MEETINGS

She saw him on the street that day.
Hi, how's it going? Pretty well.
You think the storm will head this way?
Hope not. The roof will leak like hell.

He came to her in sleep that night.
They did not touch or speak or kiss -
Ecstatic angels, borne on light,
Pinioned, unsmiling, drenched in bliss.

FOR MY FATHER

I opened up a polished box
That chimed a military air.
Lead soldiers rolled from velvet vaults -
I couldn't find you there.

I moved among the noisy crowd
On Sunday at the market place.
I thought I heard a voice like yours,
But didn't see your face.

Last night, inside my silver cup,
Still bright despite the years and wine,
I glimpsed two light and knowing eyes -
And they were yours, and mine.

Made in the USA
Lexington, KY
03 August 2012